FLUTE

2ND EDITION

THE BEST OF
The Beatles

T0053184

ISBN 978-0-7935-2142-5

HAL•LEONARD®
CORPORATION
7777 W. BLUEMOUND RD. P.O. BOX 13819 MILWAUKEE, WI 53213

Visit Hal Leonard Online at
www.halleonard.com

CONTENTS

ALL MY LOVING

Flute

Words and Music by JOHN LENNON
and PAUL McCARTNEY

ACROSS THE UNIVERSE

Flute

Words and Music by JOHN LENNON
and PAUL McCARTNEY

5

ALL YOU NEED IS LOVE

Flute

Words and Music by JOHN LENNON
and PAUL McCARTNEY

AND I LOVE HER

Flute

Words and Music by JOHN LENNON
and PAUL McCARTNEY

BACK IN THE U.S.S.R.

Flute

Words and Music by JOHN LENNON
and PAUL McCARTNEY

THE BALLAD OF JOHN AND YOKO

Flute

Words and Music by JOHN LENNON
and PAUL McCARTNEY

BECAUSE

Flute

Words and Music by JOHN LENNON
and PAUL McCARTNEY

BIRTHDAY

Flute

Words and Music by JOHN LENNON
and PAUL McCARTNEY

Moderately fast Rock

BLACKBIRD

Flute

Words and Music by JOHN LENNON
and PAUL McCARTNEY

CAN'T BUY ME LOVE

Flute

Words and Music by JOHN LENNON and PAUL McCARTNEY

COME TOGETHER

Flute

Words and Music by JOHN LENNON
and PAUL McCARTNEY

A DAY IN THE LIFE

Flute

Words and Music by JOHN LENNON
and PAUL McCARTNEY

DAY TRIPPER

Flute

Moderately

Words and Music by JOHN LENNON
and PAUL McCARTNEY

DEAR PRUDENCE

Flute

Words and Music by JOHN LENNON
and PAUL McCARTNEY

DO YOU WANT TO KNOW A SECRET?

FLUTE

Words and Music by JOHN LENNON
and PAUL McCARTNEY

DRIVE MY CAR

Flute

Words and Music by JOHN LENNON
and PAUL McCARTNEY

Moderately, with a beat

EIGHT DAYS A WEEK

Flute

Words and Music by JOHN LENNON
and PAUL McCARTNEY

ELEANOR RIGBY

Flute

Words and Music by JOHN LENNON
and PAUL McCARTNEY

EVERY LITTLE THING

Flute

Words and Music by JOHN LENNON
and PAUL McCARTNEY

THE FOOL ON THE HILL

Flute

Words and Music by JOHN LENNON
and PAUL McCARTNEY

FROM ME TO YOU

Flute

Words and Music by JOHN LENNON
and PAUL McCARTNEY

GET BACK

Flute

Words and Music by JOHN LENNON
and PAUL McCARTNEY

GIRL

FLUTE

Easy lilting beat

Words and Music by JOHN LENNON
and PAUL McCARTNEY

GOLDEN SLUMBERS

Flute

Words and Music by JOHN LENNON
and PAUL McCARTNEY

Moderately

GOOD DAY SUNSHINE

Flute

Words and Music by JOHN LENNON
and PAUL McCARTNEY

GOT TO GET YOU INTO MY LIFE

Flute

Words and Music by JOHN LENNON
and PAUL McCARTNEY

Very steady (not too fast)

A HARD DAY'S NIGHT

Flute

Words and Music by JOHN LENNON
and PAUL McCARTNEY

HELLO, GOODBYE

Flute

Words and Music by JOHN LENNON
and PAUL McCARTNEY

HELP!

Flute

Words and Music by JOHN LENNON
and PAUL McCARTNEY

HELTER SKELTER

FLUTE

Words and Music by JOHN LENNON
and PAUL McCARTNEY

HERE COMES THE SUN

Flute

Words and Music by
GEORGE HARRISON

HERE, THERE AND EVERYWHERE

Flute

Words and Music by JOHN LENNON
and PAUL McCARTNEY

HEY JUDE

FLUTE

Words and Music by JOHN LENNON
and PAUL McCARTNEY

Slowly

I FEEL FINE

Flute

Words and Music by JOHN LENNON
and PAUL McCARTNEY

I AM THE WALRUS

Flute

Words and Music by JOHN LENNON
and PAUL McCARTNEY

I SAW HER STANDING THERE

Flute

Words and Music by JOHN LENNON
and PAUL McCARTNEY

I SHOULD HAVE KNOWN BETTER

Flute

Words and Music by JOHN LENNON
and PAUL McCARTNEY

I WANT TO HOLD YOUR HAND

Flute

Words and Music by JOHN LENNON
and PAUL McCARTNEY

Moderately

1.

2.

I WILL

Flute

Words and Music by JOHN LENNON
and PAUL McCARTNEY

I'LL CRY INSTEAD

Flute

Words and Music by JOHN LENNON
and PAUL McCARTNEY

I'LL FOLLOW THE SUN

Flute

Words and Music by JOHN LENNON
and PAUL McCARTNEY

I'M A LOSER

FLUTE

Words and Music by JOHN LENNON
and PAUL McCARTNEY

I'M HAPPY JUST TO DANCE WITH YOU

Flute

Words and Music by JOHN LENNON
and PAUL McCARTNEY

Moderately

I'VE JUST SEEN A FACE

Flute

Words and Music by JOHN LENNON
and PAUL McCARTNEY

IF I FELL

Flute

Words and Music by JOHN LENNON
and PAUL McCARTNEY

IN MY LIFE

Flute

Words and Music by JOHN LENNON
and PAUL McCARTNEY

IT WON'T BE LONG

Flute

Words and Music by JOHN LENNON
and PAUL McCARTNEY

IT'S ONLY LOVE

Flute

Words and Music by JOHN LENNON
and PAUL McCARTNEY

JULIA

FLUTE

Words and Music by JOHN LENNON
and PAUL McCARTNEY

Moderately slow and wistfully

LADY MADONNA

Flute

Words and Music by JOHN LENNON
and PAUL McCARTNEY

LET IT BE

Flute

Words and Music by JOHN LENNON
and PAUL McCARTNEY

THE LONG AND WINDING ROAD

Flute

Words and Music by JOHN LENNON
and PAUL McCARTNEY

Slowly

LOVE ME DO

Flute

Words and Music by JOHN LENNON
and PAUL McCARTNEY

LUCY IN THE SKY WITH DIAMONDS

Flute

Words and Music by JOHN LENNON
and PAUL McCARTNEY

MAGICAL MYSTERY TOUR

Flute

Words and Music by JOHN LENNON
and PAUL McCARTNEY

MARTHA MY DEAR

FLUTE

Words and Music by JOHN LENNON
and PAUL McCARTNEY

MICHELLE

Flute

Words and Music by JOHN LENNON
and PAUL McCARTNEY

NO REPLY

Flute

Words and Music by JOHN LENNON
and PAUL McCARTNEY

NORWEGIAN WOOD

(This Bird Has Flown)

Flute

Words and Music by JOHN LENNON
and PAUL McCARTNEY

NOWHERE MAN

Flute

Words and Music by JOHN LENNON
and PAUL McCARTNEY

OB-LA-DI, OB-LA-DA

Flute

Words and Music by JOHN LENNON
and PAUL McCARTNEY

OCTOPUS'S GARDEN

Flute

Words and Music by RICHARD STARKEY,
JOHN LENNON and PAUL McCARTNEY

Moderately bright

PAPERBACK WRITER

Flute

Words and Music by JOHN LENNON
and PAUL McCARTNEY

Bright Rock

PENNY LANE

FLUTE

Words and Music by JOHN LENNON
and PAUL McCARTNEY

PLEASE PLEASE ME

Flute

Words and Music by JOHN LENNON
and PAUL McCARTNEY

P.S. I LOVE YOU

Flute

Words and Music by JOHN LENNON
and PAUL McCARTNEY

Moderate Rock

REVOLUTION

Flute

Words and Music by JOHN LENNON
and PAUL McCARTNEY

RUN FOR YOUR LIFE

Flute

Words and Music by JOHN LENNON
and PAUL McCARTNEY

SGT. PEPPER'S LONELY HEARTS CLUB BAND

Flute

Words and Music by JOHN LENNON
and PAUL McCARTNEY

SHE LOVES YOU

Flute

Words and Music by JOHN LENNON
and PAUL McCARTNEY

SHE'S A WOMAN

Flute

Words and Music by JOHN LENNON
and PAUL McCARTNEY

SOMETHING

Flute

Words and Music by
GEORGE HARRISON

STRAWBERRY FIELDS FOREVER

Flute

Words and Music by JOHN LENNON
and PAUL McCARTNEY

TELL ME WHY

Flute

Words and Music by JOHN LENNON
and PAUL McCARTNEY

THANK YOU GIRL

Flute

Words and Music by JOHN LENNON
and PAUL McCARTNEY

THINGS WE SAID TODAY

Flute

Words and Music by JOHN LENNON
and PAUL McCARTNEY

Moderately fast

THIS BOY
(Ringo's Theme)

Flute

Words and Music by JOHN LENNON
and PAUL McCARTNEY

TICKET TO RIDE

Flute

Words and Music by JOHN LENNON
and PAUL McCARTNEY

Moderate Rock

TWIST AND SHOUT

Flute

Words and Music by BERT RUSSELL
and PHIL MEDLEY

WE CAN WORK IT OUT

Flute

Words and Music by JOHN LENNON
and PAUL McCARTNEY

WHEN I'M SIXTY-FOUR

Flute

Words and Music by JOHN LENNON
and PAUL McCARTNEY

WHILE MY GUITAR GENTLY WEEPS

FLUTE

Words and Music by
GEORGE HARRISON

Moderately

WITH A LITTLE HELP FROM MY FRIENDS

Flute

Words and Music by JOHN LENNON
and PAUL McCARTNEY

THE WORD

Flute

Words and Music by JOHN LENNON
and PAUL McCARTNEY

YELLOW SUBMARINE

Flute

Words and Music by JOHN LENNON
and PAUL McCARTNEY

March tempo

YES IT IS

Flute

Words and Music by JOHN LENNON
and PAUL McCARTNEY

YESTERDAY

Flute

Words and Music by JOHN LENNON
and PAUL McCARTNEY

YOU CAN'T DO THAT

Flute

Words and Music by JOHN LENNON
and PAUL McCARTNEY

YOU WON'T SEE ME

Flute

Words and Music by JOHN LENNON
and PAUL McCARTNEY

Moderately

YOU'RE GOING TO LOSE THAT GIRL

Flute

Words and Music by JOHN LENNON
and PAUL McCARTNEY

Moderately

YOU'VE GOT TO HIDE YOUR LOVE AWAY

Flute

Words and Music by JOHN LENNON
and PAUL McCARTNEY

Moderately

YOUR MOTHER SHOULD KNOW

Flute

Words and Music by JOHN LENNON
and PAUL McCARTNEY